LEISURE ARTS PRESENTS

QUICK COZY FLANNEL QUILTS

Compiled and edited by Rhonda Richards

Quick Cozy Flannel Quilts

©1999 by Oxmoor House, Inc.

Book Division of Southern Progress Corporation

P.O. Box 2463, Birmingham, Alabama 35201

Published by Oxmoor House, Inc., and Leisure Arts, Inc.

Library of Congress Catalog Card Number: 99-71764

Softcover ISBN: 0-8487-1948-4

Manufactured in the United States of America

Seventh Printing 2002

Editor-in-Chief: Nancy Fitzpatrick Wyatt
Senior Crafts Editor: Susan Ramey Cleveland
Senior Editor, Copy and Homes: Olivia Kindig Wells
Art Director: James Boone

Quick Cozy Flannel Quilts

Editor: Rhonda Richards
Assistant Editor: Lauren Caswell Brooks
Contributing Technical Writer: Laura Morris Edwards
Copy Editor: L. Amanda Owens
Associate Art Director: Cynthia R. Cooper
Contributing Designer: Carol Damsky
Illustrator: Kelly Davis
Senior Photographer: John O'Hagan
Photo Stylist: Linda Baltzell Wright
Director, Production and Distribution: Phillip Lee
Associate Production Manager: Theresa L. Beste
Production Assistant: Faye Porter Bonner

We're Here for You!

We at Oxmoor House are dedicated to serving you with reliable information that expands your imagination and enriches your life. We welcome your comments and suggestions.

Please write us at:

Oxmoor House

Editor, *Quick Cozy Flannel Quilts*

2100 Lakeshore Drive

Birmingham, AL 35209

To order additional publications, call 1-800-633-4910.

From the Editor

When flannels first became popular a few years ago, I started my collection with a sackful purchased at the International Quilt Festival in Houston, Texas. The masculine-looking prints seemed the perfect choice for making my husband a quilt (see *Buzz Saw* on page 8).

I get home from work about an hour before my husband does. A year ago, I used that time to work secretly on his quilt each day. I'll never forget the look on his face when he opened the attractively wrapped package on Christmas Day and exclaimed, "When did *this* happen?" We keep the quilt right by the couch, and he naps under it often.

Since I made that quilt, even more flannels have appeared on the market. In addition to masculine plaids, my collection now contains feminine florals, pastel plaids, solids, and even a few novelty prints. Flannels suitable for any look are now available, from traditional to contemporary.

Our goal in selecting projects for this book was to offer you a variety of easy-to-make quilts especially suited for use with flannel fabrics. You'll find rotary-cutting instructions, as well as tips to help you complete your quilt quickly and successfully.

If you like the look of diamonds but thought they were too hard to cut and piece, try the rotary-cutting shortcut used in *Diamond Four-Patch* on page 60. You'll be surprised how quickly you can make blocks for that quilt. If you enjoy both piecing and appliquéing, then our cover quilt, *Family Memories* (page 12), is ideal for you. Looking for a portable project that you can work on while waiting in a doctor's office or at soccer practice? Try *Grandmother's Flower Garden* on page 52.

Even if you're like me and only have an hour—or less—a day to devote to quilting, you can take advantage of these techniques to make quick, cozy flannel quilts for yourself and for someone you love.

Rhonda Richards

Contents

◆ ◆ ◆

Projects

Page 36

Page 20

Page 12

Page 48

Techniques

Tips for Working with Flannels

Some quilters experience "flannel phobia," because they think that working with flannel differs from using regular 100% cotton. While that's true, the differences are positive ones. The following tips come from quilters featured in this book, as well as from flannel manufacturers themselves.

- **Buy good-quality flannel from brand-name manufacturers.** Cheap flannel will pill as you work with it, so imagine how much it will pill as the quilt gets loved and washed. Quality flannel is worth the few extra dollars. Two large manufacturers include Benartex and Moda. See Resources on page 64 for mail-order sources.

- **Do not prewash the fabric.** It will get extremely soft in the wash and may become limp. You don't want to have to starch the softness out afterwards in order to work with it. Don't worry about shrinkage when you wash the quilt; use 100% cotton batting, and the materials can all shrink together and give the quilt a soft, textured look.

- **Take advantage of the fact that you may not need to use pins** when working with flannel, because the fuzzy pieces tend to stick together as you sew.

- **Use a sharp rotary blade.** If you haven't treated yourself to an extralarge rotary cutter yet, do it. You'll love how it slices through multiple layers of flannel.

- **Remember that flannel does have more stretch** or give than regular 100% cotton fabric. This can be a bonus if your blocks aren't exactly even and you need to stretch a piece slightly to make it fit. A little care when handling the fabric will prevent excess stretching.

- **Machine-quilt flannel quilts.** Since the layers are so thick, fine hand stitching is difficult to do. You can purchase a walking foot and machine-quilt the quilt yourself or send it to a professional machine quilter. Ask local quilt shops for the name of a professional quilter.

- **Try utility quilting.** If you enjoy handquilting, this is the option for you. You'll need a large-eyed needle and pearl cotton thread. In utility quilting, you actually *want* your stitches to be large and visible! Make ¼"-long stitches, spaced about ¼" apart. This adds a folk-art look to your quilt. You can either pop the knots inside as usual or leave them on the front or the back for a primitive look.

- **Keep in mind that the quilting shows up better after you wash the quilt.** Since the flannel and the batting shrink together in the wash (and the shrinking is usually only slight), the quilting becomes more visible, giving the quilt a more traditional look afterward.

FABRIC BY BENARTEX

Bias Binding

Since flannel has a lot of "give" to begin with, you may want to use straight-grain binding for most of your quilts. However, you should use bias binding when you have rounded corners, as in *Star Burst* (page 20) or *Churn Dash* (page 16), or when you want a plaid binding on point. (See page 59 for straight-grain binding instructions.)

1. To cut bias binding, start with a square. (For queen-size quilt, 32"-square is sufficient, so you should usually never need more than 1 yard of fabric.) At top and bottom edges, center pins with heads toward **inside.** At each side, center pins with heads toward **outside** edges.
2. Cut square in half diagonally to make 2 triangles.

3. With right sides facing, match edges with pin heads pointed to **outside.** Remove pins and join triangles with ¼" seam. Press seam open.
4. On wrong side of fabric, mark cutting lines parallel to long edges. For most flannel quilts, you'll want 2½"-wide binding strip. (For other fabrics, 2¼" is sufficient.) Draw lines 2½" apart.

5. With right sides facing, match edges with pin heads pointed to **inside,** offsetting 1 width of binding strip as shown. Join edges with ¼" seam to make tube. Press seam open.
6. Begin cutting at extended edge, using fabric shears. Follow drawn lines, rolling tube as you cut, until all fabric is cut into a continuous strip.

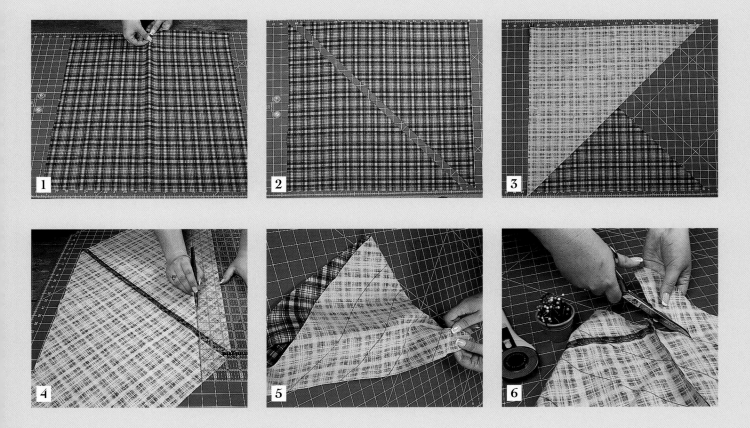

THIS QUILT IS BASED ON A DESIGN BY MARTHA THOMPSON FROM HER BOOK, *START WITH SQUARES* (THAT PATCHWORK PLACE).

Buzz Saw

*F*lannels are a natural choice for making quilts for men and boys. Tim Wamble's wife, Rhonda, chose the woodsy background fabric to make a quilt for her Eagle Scout husband. By piecing block units into the border, the Buzz Saws appear to spin off the quilt!

Finished Size: 60" x 75"
Blocks: 56 (7½") Buzz Saw Blocks

MATERIALS

10 fat quarters* (or 2¼ yards total) coordinating dark prints and plaids for blocks
7½ yards light theme print for blocks, border, and backing
1 yard brown plaid for inner border and binding (1½ yards for unpieced borders)
Twin-size batting
*Fat quarter = 18" x 22"

CUTTING

Measurements include ¼" seam allowances. Cut selvage to selvage, unless otherwise noted.

From each dark fat quarter, cut:
- 3 (8⅜") squares. Cut squares in half diagonally to make 60 half-square triangles for blocks. You will have 4 extra.
- 6 (2" x 8") rectangles. You will have 4 extra.

From light theme print, cut:
- 4½ yards for backing.
- 1½ yards. Cut into 5 (6½"-wide) lengthwise strips. Cut strips into:
  - 4 (6½" x 16") strips,
  - 2 (6½" x 31") strips,
  - and 2 (6½" x 46") strips for outer border.

- 6 (8⅜"-wide) selvage to selvage strips. Cut strips into 28 (8⅜") squares. Cut squares in half diagonally to make 56 half-square triangles for blocks.

From brown plaid, cut:
- 6 (2"-wide) strips. Cut strips into 4 (2" x 16") strips, 2 (2" x 31") strips, and 2 (2" x 46") strips for inner border. Piece as needed. If you prefer unpieced borders, cut 5 (2"-wide) lengthwise strips from alternate yardage. Cut strips into lengths above.
- 7 (2¼"-wide) strips for binding [or 6 (2¼"-wide) lengthwise strips, if you cut lengthwise borders].

BLOCK ASSEMBLY

1. Join 1 light half-square triangle and 1 dark half-square triangle to make 1 square *(Diagram 1)*. Make 56 squares.

2. With dark triangle in lower right corner, cut each square into 4 (2"-wide) strips as shown in *Diagram 2*.

3. Mix strips as desired. Join 4 assorted strips as shown in *Diagram 3* to form saw unit. Join 1 (2" x 8") dark rectangle to dark side of block to complete *(Diagram 4)*.

4. Make 56 Buzz Saw blocks.

Diagram 1

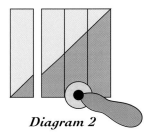

Diagram 2

Diagram 3

Diagram 4

Quilt Assembly

1. Lay out blocks in 8 horizontal rows of 6 blocks each, as shown in *Quilt Top Assembly Diagram.* Join into rows; join rows to complete center. You will have 8 blocks left for border.

2. Join 1 (2" x 16") brown plaid strip to 1 (6½" x 16") light border strip (Set A). Join 1 (2" x 31") brown plaid strip to 1 (6½" x 31") light border strip (Set B). Join 2 Buzz Saw blocks as shown.

3. Join 1 Set A to left end of block unit as shown. Join 1 Set B to right end of block unit.

4. Repeat steps 2 and 3 to make 2 top and bottom border strips. Repeat, using remaining 46"-long border strips for B strips in side borders.

5. Join border strips to appropriate sides of quilt, aligning block units as shown. Miter corners.

Quilting and Finishing

1. Divide backing fabric into 2 (2¼-yard) lengths. Cut 1 piece in half lengthwise. Sew 1 narrow panel to 1 side of wide panel. Press seam allowances toward narrow panel. Remaining panel is extra and may be used to make a hanging sleeve.

2. Layer backing, batting, and quilt top; baste. Quilt as desired. Quilt shown was meander-quilted in the light areas and features a fleur-de-lis motif in the dark areas.

3. Join 2¼"-wide brown plaid strips into 1 continuous piece for straight-grain French-fold binding. Add binding to quilt.

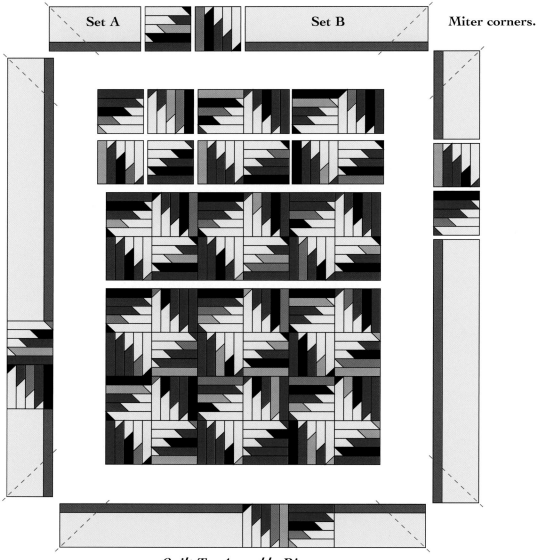

Quilt Top Assembly Diagram

Family Memories

oni Foster began this quilt to incorporate one of her dad's flannel shirts. "My dad wore it for several years," says Toni, "and when he died, my mom continued to enjoy its warmth. Both of my parents have now passed away, and I wanted to preserve the shirt and the memories associated with it." Toni gave the quilt to her sister, Janet Rash, for Christmas.

QUILT BY TONI FOSTER; OWNED BY JANET RASH; BORDER PATTERNS BY LIZ PORTER

MATERIALS

9 fat eighths* light prints for blocks
12 to 15 fat eighths* dark prints
1 yard green print
1 fat eighth* solid red for cherries
¼ yard solid green for inner border
1½ yards tan for appliquéd border
5¼ yards red print for outer border,
    backing, and binding
Twin-size batting
*Fat eighth = 9" x 22"

CUTTING

Instructions are for a two-color block. Mix or match fabrics as desired or refer to photo for inspiration. Measurements include ¼" seam allowances. Cut selvage to selvage, unless otherwise noted.

From each light print, cut:
• 2 (2½") A squares for center.
• 1 (2½") A square for background.
• 4 (2½" x 4½") B rectangles for background.
• 1 (4⅞") square for background. Cut square in half diagonally to make 2 half-square triangles (D). You will have 1 extra.

From assorted dark prints, cut:
• 9 sets of 4 (2½") A squares for points and 1 (2⅞") square to match. Cut (2⅞") square in half diagonally to make 2 C half-square triangles.
• 9 sets of 2 (2½") A squares for center. These may match or contrast with point fabric.
• 18 (6⅝") squares. Cut squares in half diagonally to make 36 half-square triangles (E).

• 4 birds and 4 reversed birds.
• 8 wings.
• 8 flowers and 8 flower centers.
• 8 tulips and 8 tulip tips.
• 4 baskets and 4 hearts.

From green print, cut:
• 1 (18"-wide) strip. From this, cut 8 (1⅛"-wide) bias strips to make 8 (22"-long) strips for vines.
• 48 leaves.

From solid red, cut:
• 40 cherries.

From solid green, cut:
• 4 (2"-wide) strips. Cut strips into 2 (2" x 34½") top and bottom borders and 2 (2" x 37½") side borders.

From tan, cut:
• 4 (7½"-wide) lengthwise strips. Cut strips into 2 (7½" x 37½") top and bottom borders and 2 (7½" x 51½") side borders.

From red print, cut:
• 3½ yards for backing.
• 4 (3½"-wide) lengthwise strips. Cut strips into 2 (3½" x 51½") side borders and 2 (3½" x 57½") top and bottom borders.

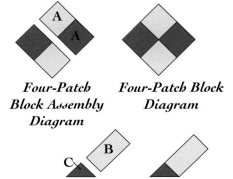

Four-Patch Block Assembly Diagram

Four-Patch Block Diagram

B/C Assembly Diagrams

• From remainder, cut 4 (2¼"-wide) lengthwise strips for binding.

BLOCK ASSEMBLY

Refer to *Block Assembly Diagram* throughout.

1. Join 1 light A and 1 dark A as shown in *Four-Patch Block Assembly Diagram*. Repeat. Join A units to make center Four-Patch Unit (*Four-Patch Block Diagram*).

2. Referring to *Diagonal Seams Diagrams*, place 1 dark A square atop 1 light B rectangle. Stitch on diagonal, trim, and press open. Repeat on opposite end to make 1 Goose Chase unit. Make 2 Goose Chase units.

3. Join 1 dark C triangle to 1 end of 1 light B rectangle. Repeat for opposite side (*B/C Assembly Diagrams*).

4. Referring to *Block Assembly Diagram*, join 1 Goose Chase unit to 1 side of center unit. Join 1 light A to remaining Goose Chase unit; join to center unit. Join 1 B/C unit to each side. Add 1 light D triangle to bottom to complete 1 Basket block.

5. Add 1 E triangle to each side of block (*Setting Diagram*, page 14).

6. Make 9 basket blocks (*Block Diagram*, page 14).

Diagonal Seams Diagrams

Block Assembly Diagram

QUILT ASSEMBLY

1. Lay out blocks in 3 horizontal rows of 3 blocks each, as shown in *Quilt Top Assembly Diagram.* Join into rows; join rows to complete center.

2. Measure quilt to ensure that borders will fit. Trim if necessary. Add solid green 2" x 34½" borders to top and bottom of quilt. Add solid green 2" x 37½" borders to sides of quilt.

3. Add tan 7½" x 37½" borders to top and bottom of quilt. Add tan 7½" x 51½" borders to sides of quilt.

4. Add red print 3½" x 51½" borders to sides of quilt. Add red print 3½" x 57½" borders to top and bottom of quilt.

5. Appliqué tan border as shown in photo with 8 vines, 4 baskets, 48 leaves, 4 hearts, 4 birds, 4 reversed birds, 8 wings, 8 flowers and 8 flower centers, 8 tulips and 8 tulip tips, and 40 cherries.

QUILTING AND FINISHING

1. Divide backing fabric into 2 (1¾-yard) lengths. Cut 1 piece in half lengthwise. Sew 1 narrow panel to 1 side of wide panel. Press seam allowances toward narrow panel. Remaining panel is extra and may be used for hanging sleeve.

2. Layer backing, batting, and quilt top; baste. Quilt as desired. Quilt shown was utility-quilted in a partial grid in blocks, in diagonals in setting triangles, and outline-quilted with hearts in appliquéd border.

3. Join 2¼"-wide red print strips into 1 continuous piece for straight-grain French-fold binding. Add binding to quilt.

Setting Diagram

Block Diagram

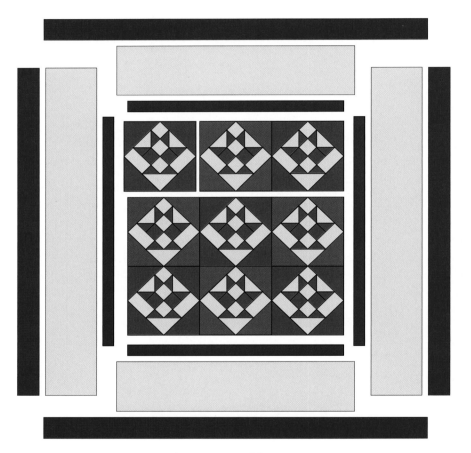

Quilt Top Assembly Diagram

Appliqué shapes at right were designed by Liz Porter and appear in **Quick Quilts from the Heart** *by Oxmoor House.*

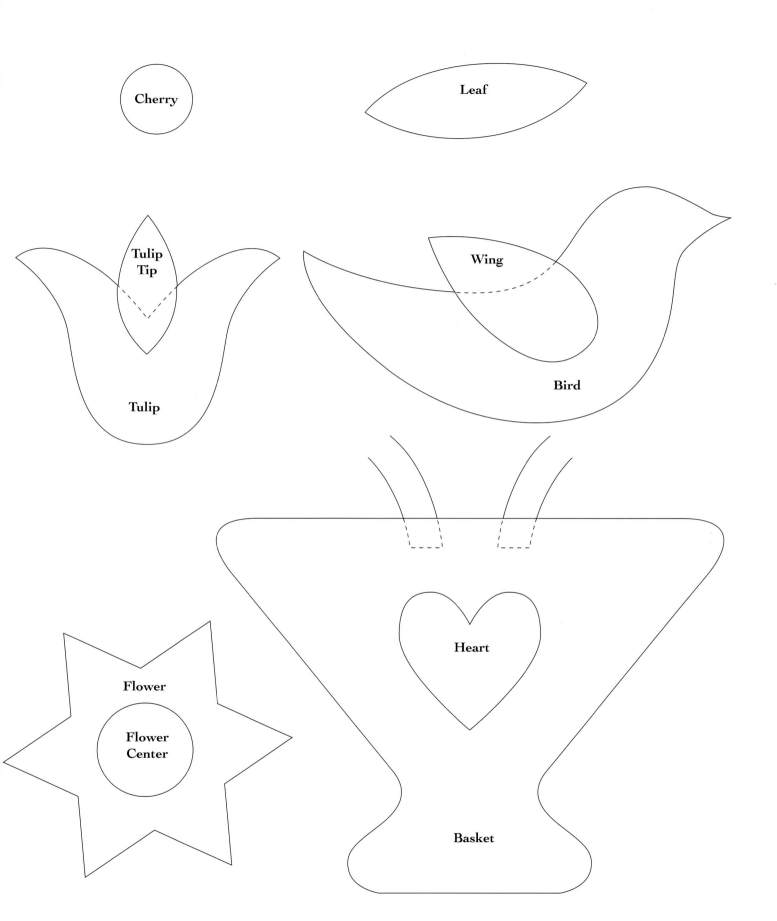

Cherry

Leaf

Tulip Tip

Tulip

Wing

Bird

Flower

Flower Center

Heart

Basket

Quilt by Cheryl Gratt

Churn Dash

*Y*ou may recognize this traditional pattern by one of its other names: *Monkey Wrench, Hole in the Barn Door, Old Mill,* or *Love Knot.* Depending on your fabric choices, most time-honored blocks can be made into masculine or feminine quilts.

Finished Size: 76" x 76"
Blocks: 13 (12") Churn Dash Blocks

MATERIALS

39 fat eighths* (or 3 yards total) assorted medium and dark fabrics for blocks
1¼ yards light brown for sashing
1½ yards floral for setting triangles
1¾ yards solid burgundy for inner border and binding (2 yards for unpieced borders)
1¼ yards green plaid for outer border and sashing squares (2¼ yards for unpieced borders)
4½ yards dark stripe for backing
Full-size batting
*Fat eighth = 9" x 22"

CUTTING

Measurements include ¼" seam allowances. Cut selvage to selvage, unless otherwise noted.

From assorted medium and dark fabrics, choose 3. Cut:
- Fabric 1:
  - 1 (4½") square for center (C).
  - 2 (4⅞") squares. Cut squares in half diagonally to make 4 half-square triangles (A).

- **Fabric 2:**
  - 4 (2½" x 4½") rectangles (B).
- **Fabric 3:**
  - 4 (2½" x 4½") rectangles (B).
  - 2 (4⅞") squares. Cut squares in half diagonally to make 4 half-square triangles (A).
- Repeat to cut 13 sets.

From light brown, cut:
- 12 (3"-wide) strips. Cut strips into 36 (3" x 12½") rectangles for sashing.

From floral, cut:
- 1 (22"-wide) lengthwise strip. Cut strip into 2 (22") squares. Cut squares in quarters diagonally to make 8 side setting triangles.
- 1 (13"-wide) lengthwise strip. Cut strip into 2 (13") squares. Cut squares in half diagonally to make 4 corner setting triangles.

From solid burgundy, cut:
- 8 (3"-wide) strips. Piece to make 2 (3" x 66") side borders and 2 (3" x 71") top and bottom borders. If you prefer unpieced borders, cut 4 (3"-wide) lengthwise strips from alternate yardage. Trim borders to above lengths.

- 1 (30") square for bias binding. If you prefer to leave corners square, cut 4 (2¼"-wide) lengthwise strips for straight grain French-fold binding.

From green plaid, cut:
- 8 (3½"-wide) strips. Piece to make 2 (3½" x 71") side borders and 2 (3½" x 77") top and bottom borders. If you prefer unpieced borders, cut 4 (3½"-wide) lengthwise strips from alternate yardage. Trim borders to above lengths.
- 2 (3"-wide) strips. Cut strips into 24 (3") squares for sashing squares.

A Unit Assembly Diagrams

B Unit Assembly Diagrams

BLOCK ASSEMBLY

1. Join 1 dark (Fabric 1) A and 1 background (Fabric 3) A to make 1 A unit (*A Unit Assembly Diagrams, page 17*). Make 4 matching A units.

2. Join 1 background (Fabric 3) B and 1 medium (Fabric 2) B to make 1 B unit (*B Unit Assembly Diagrams, page 17*). Make 4 matching B units.

3. Lay out A units, B units, and 1 C as shown in *Block Assembly Diagram*. Join into rows; join rows to complete block (*Block Diagram*).

4. Make 13 Churn Dash blocks.

QUILT ASSEMBLY

1. Lay out blocks, sashing strips, sashing squares, and setting triangles as shown in *Quilt Top Assembly Diagram*. Join into diagonal rows. Join rows to complete center.

2. Join 1 (3" x 66") burgundy border strip to each side of quilt. Join remaining burgundy strips to top and bottom.

3. Join 1 (3½" x 71") green plaid side border strip to each side of quilt. Join remaining green plaid strips to top and bottom.

QUILTING AND FINISHING

1. Divide backing fabric into 2 (2¼-yard) lengths. Cut 1 piece in half lengthwise. Sew 1 narrow panel to each side of wide panel. Press seam allowances toward narrow panels.

2. Layer backing, batting, and quilt top; baste. Quilt as desired. Quilt shown has allover large-scale meander quilting. Round corners, if desired.

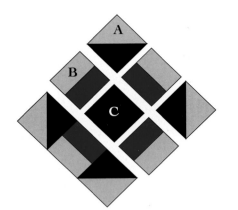

Block Assembly Diagram

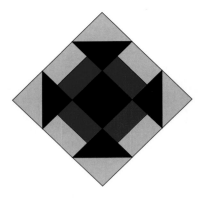

Block Diagram

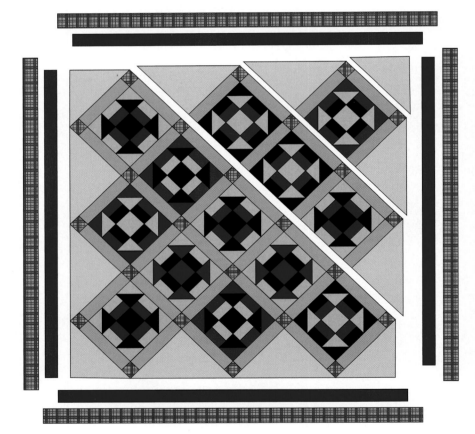

Quilt Top Assembly Diagram

3. Make 7 yards of 2¼"-wide French-fold bias binding. Add binding to quilt. For straight grain binding, join 2¼"-wide burgundy strips into 1 continuous piece to make binding. Add binding to quilt.

Star Burst

urn a simple Ohio Star block into a spectacular Star Burst block by making pieced units for the corners. Use flannel scraps or fat-eighth bundles to make this quilt. You can leave the border corners square or round them, as in this quilt.

Finished Size: 54" x 68"
Blocks: 12 (12") Star Burst Blocks

MATERIALS

12 fat eighths* assorted dark fabrics
for star
1¼ yards light for star background
1¾ yards dark blue for sashing and
binding
¼ yard rust print for sashing squares
1 yard blue print for border (or 2
yards for unpieced borders)
4 yards green print for backing
Twin-size batting
*Fat eighth = 9" x 22"

CUTTING

Measurements include ¼" seam
allowances. Cut selvage to selvage,
unless otherwise noted.

From each dark fat eighth, cut:
- 2 (5¼") squares. Cut squares in
quarters diagonally to make 8
quarter-square triangles (C).
- 1 (4½") square (D).
- 4 (2⅞") squares. Cut squares in
half diagonally to make 8 half-
square triangles (A).
- 4 (2½") squares (B).

From light, cut:
- 4 (2⅞"-wide) strips. Cut strips into
48 (2⅞") squares. Cut squares in
half diagonally to make 96 half-
square triangles (A).
- 3 (5¼"-wide) strips. Cut strips into
24 (5¼") squares. Cut squares in
quarters diagonally to make 96
quarter-square triangles (C).
- 3 (2½"-wide) strips. Cut strips into
48 (2½") squares (B).

From dark blue, cut:
- 11 (2½"-wide) strips. Cut strips
into 31 (2½" x 12½") rectangles
for sashing strips.
- 1 (27") square for binding. If you
prefer to leave corners square, cut
7 (2¼"-wide) strips for straight-
grain binding.

From rust print, cut:
- 2 (2½"-wide) strips. Cut strips into
20 (2½") squares for sashing
squares.

From blue print, cut:
- 6 (5½"-wide) strips. Cut strips into
2 (5½" x 44½") top and bottom
borders and 2 (5½" x 68½") side
borders. Piece as needed. If you
prefer unpieced borders, cut 4
(5½"-wide) lengthwise strips from
alternate yardage. Trim borders to
above lengths.

BLOCK ASSEMBLY

1. Choose 1 D and 4 B squares in 1
fabric for Fabric 1. Choose 8 Cs and
8 As in another fabric for Fabric 2.
2. Join 1 light A and 1 dark A to
make 1 A square *(A Unit Diagram)*.
Repeat. Join with 1 light B and 1
dark B as shown in *A/B Unit Assembly
Diagram* to make 1 A unit. Repeat to
make 4 A units *(A/B Unit Diagram)*.
3. Referring to *C Unit Assembly
Diagrams*, join 1 light C and 1 dark C
to make 1 half-square unit. Repeat.
Join as shown to make 1 C unit.
Repeat to make 4 C units.
4. Lay out 4 A units, 4 C units, and
1 D square as shown in *Block
Assembly Diagram*. Join units into
rows; join rows to complete 1 block
(Block Diagram).
5. Make 12 Star Burst blocks.

*A Unit
Diagram*

*A/B Unit Assembly
Diagram*

A/B Unit Diagram

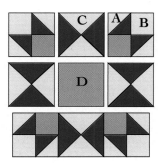
C Unit Assembly Diagrams

Block Assembly Diagram

Block Diagram

QUILT ASSEMBLY

1. Referring to *Sashing Row Assembly Diagram*, alternate and join 3 sashing strips and 4 sashing squares to make 1 Sashing Row. Make 5 Sashing Rows.

2. Referring to *Block Row Assembly Diagram*, alternate and join 3 blocks and 4 sashing strips to make 1 Block Row. Make 4 Block Rows.

3. Using photo as a guide, alternate sashing rows and block rows as shown. Join to complete quilt center.

4. Join 1 (5½" x 44½") blue print border strip to top and bottom of quilt. Join 1 (5½" x 68½") blue print border strip to each side of quilt.

QUILTING AND FINISHING

1. Divide backing fabric into 2 (2-yard) lengths. Cut 1 piece in half lengthwise. Sew 1 narrow panel to 1 side of wide panel. Press seam allowances toward narrow panel. Remaining panel is extra and may be used to make hanging sleeve.

2. Layer backing, batting, and quilt top; baste. Quilt as desired. Quilt shown was meander-quilted in light areas and has interlocking pattern in border.

3. To make rounded corners, use Corner Pattern at right to trim corners of quilt into quarter circles.

4. Make 7 yards of 2¼"-wide bias binding from 27" dark blue square. Add binding to quilt. If you prefer to leave corners square, join 2¼"-wide dark blue strips into 1 continuous piece for straight-grain French-fold binding. Add binding to quilt.

Sashing Row Assembly Diagram

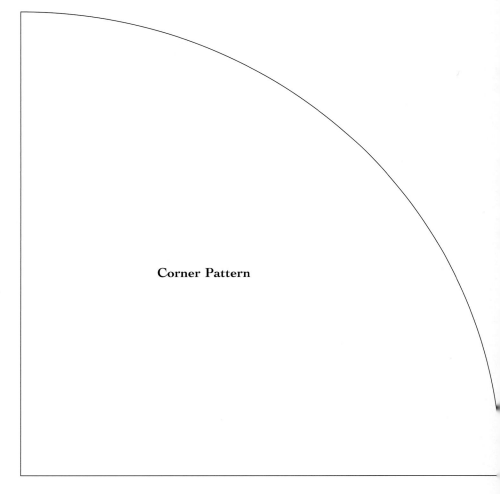

Block Row Assembly Diagram

Corner Pattern

Snake in the Hollow

*U*sing monofilament thread to machine-appliqué these fan units makes quick work of a traditionally time-consuming pattern. And the thread becomes nearly invisible on the thick flannel. If you're working with dark fabrics, such as the ones shown here, look for a smoky-colored thread instead of a clear one.

QUILT BY CINDY COOPER; QUILTED BY NEW TRADITIONS

Finished Size: 69½" x 81½"
Blocks: 30 (12") Fan Blocks

MATERIALS

6½ yards total assorted plaids for
blocks

5 yards solid brown for backing and
border

1¼ yards red-and-brown plaid for
outer border

Twin-size batting

CUTTING

Measurements include ¼" seam
allowances. Cut selvage to selvage,
unless otherwise noted. Border strips
are exact length needed. You may
want to cut them longer to allow for
piecing variations.

From assorted plaids, cut:
• 30 (12½") squares for block
backgrounds.
• 180 As.
• 30 Bs.

From solid brown, cut:
• 2 (2½-yard) lengths for backing.
• From 1 backing length, cut 4
(1¼"-wide) lengthwise strips for
inner border. Trim strips to make 2
(1¼" x 72½") side borders and 2
(1¼" x 62") top and bottom inner
borders.

From red-and-brown plaid, cut:
• 8 (4½"-wide) strips. Piece strips to
make 2 (4½" x 74") side borders
and 2 (4½" x 70") top and bottom
borders.

BLOCK ASSEMBLY

1. Join 2 As along sides to make a
pair. Do not stitch beyond top dots.
Make 3 A pairs *(Fan Assembly*

Diagram). Join pairs to form fan *(Fan
Unit Diagram)*.

2. Appliqué fan to 1 corner of 1
background block. Appliqué 1 B
quarter circle to fan *(Block Diagram)*.
Trim background fabric behind
applique, leaving ¼" seam allowance.
This completes 1 Fan block.

3. Make 30 Fan blocks.

*Fan Assembly
Diagram*

*Fan Unit
Diagram*

Block Diagram

Using Monofilament Thread

If you have never used monofilament
thread in your sewing machine, plan
to spend about 30 minutes tinkering
with the dials to get the tension and
the setting adjusted correctly. Sewing
machines don't respond to this special
thread the same way they do to other
types of thread. Use the tips below to
get started.

• **Loosen the top tension.** Monofilament thread tends to put more
stress on the machine's parts. You will
know that the tension is too tight if the
bobbin thread makes small loops on
the top of the fabric. If this happens,
loosen the top tension and try again.

• **Match the bobbin thread to your
foundation fabric.** The bobbin thread
still may peek through once in a while,
so you'll want it to match the fabric.

• **Do not put monofilament thread
in the bobbin;** it will cause all kinds of
problems and may harm your machine.

• **Adjust your machine to .5 stitch
length.** Turn the flywheel by hand one
turn so that the top thread catches the
bottom thread. Pull the bobbin thread
to the top. Take about 3 to 5 stitches
to lock the threads and then trim the
thread tails.

• **Now adjust your stitch length to
1.5** and set the machine for a blindhem stitch.

• **Stitch** so that the straight lines fall
just to the outside of the appliqué and
the V catches the edge of the shape
(Blindhem Diagram).

*Blindhem
Diagram*

• **To turn corners,** stop with the needle down in the fabric, raise the presser foot, and pivot the fabric. Lower
the presser foot and continue stitching.

• **To end stitching,** lock the stitches
by setting the stitch length to .5
during the final few stitches. Trim the
thread tails.

Every machine is different, so experi-
ment with your machine's settings.
When you are happy with the results,
write down the numbers for the tension, the stitch width, and the stitch
length so that you won't have to test
your machine the next time you use
monofilament thread.

QUILT ASSEMBLY

1. Lay out blocks in 6 horizontal rows of 5 blocks each, as shown in *Quilt Top Assembly Diagram*. Join into rows; join rows to complete center.

2. Measure quilt to ensure that borders will fit; trim if necessary. Add 1¼" x 72½" solid brown borders to sides of quilt. Add 1¼" x 62" solid brown borders to top and bottom of quilt.

3. Add 4½" x 74" red-and-brown plaid borders to sides of quilt. Add 4½" x 70" red-and-brown plaid borders to top and bottom of quilt.

QUILTING AND FINISHING

1. Join backing panels lengthwise to make backing.

2. Layer backing, batting, and quilt top; baste. Quilt as desired. Quilt shown was quilted in allover leaf pattern.

3. Trim backing to 2" all around. Fold in 1"; fold to front and slipstitch to form binding. Miter corners.

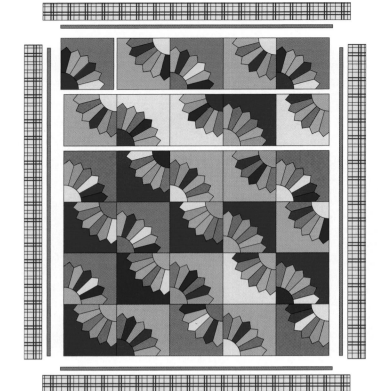

Quilt Top Assembly Diagram

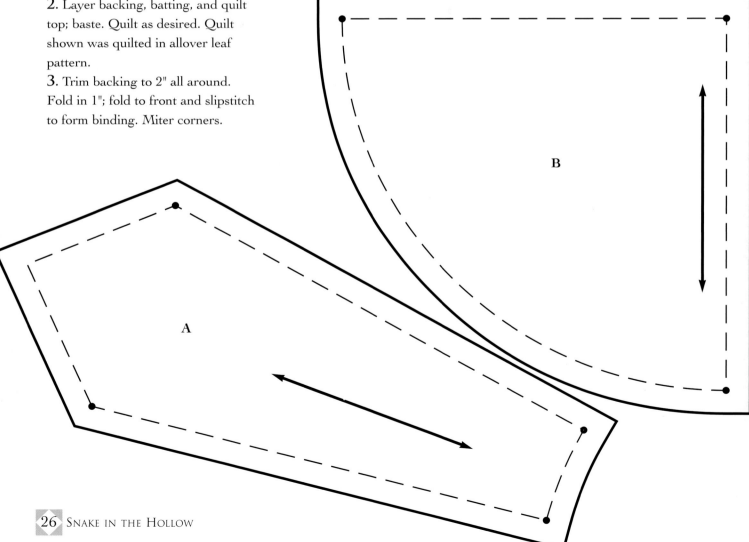

Old Maid's Puzzle

This quilt was Lena Colley's first experience working with flannel. "I fell in love with a flannel bundle a friend brought me back from Houston, Texas. I knew I had to make a flannel quilt," says Lena. She also notes that this was the first time she'd seen floral flannels on the market.

MATERIALS

¾ yard solid black for block points

¼ yard black-and-tan plaid for
blocks

1 yard solid tan for background and
border

4¾ yards black floral print for
blocks, border, binding, and
backing

Twin-size batting

CUTTING

Measurements include ¼" seam
allowances. Cut fabric selvage to
selvage, unless otherwise noted.
Border strips are exact length needed. You may want to cut them longer
to allow for piecing variations.

From solid black, cut:

• 6 (2⅞"-wide) strips. Cut strips into
80 (2⅞") squares. Cut squares in
half diagonally to make 160 half-
square triangles A. If you prefer
quick-piecing half-square triangles,
cut 6 (2⅞"-wide) strips and set
aside.

From black-and-tan plaid, cut:

• 3 (2½"-wide) strips. Cut strips into
40 (2½") squares (B).

From solid tan, cut:

• 6 (2⅞"-wide) strips. Cut strips into
80 (2⅞") squares. Cut squares in
half diagonally to make 160 half-
square triangles A. If you prefer
quick-piecing half-square triangles,
cut 6 (2⅞"-wide) strips and set
aside.

• 3 (2½"-wide) strips. Cut strips into
40 (2½") squares (B).

• 4 (1½"-wide) strips. Cut strips into
2 (1½" x 32½") top and bottom
border strips and 2 (1½" x 42½")
side border strips.

From black floral print, cut:

• 3 yards for backing.

• 1¾ yards. Cut 4 (6½"-wide)
lengthwise strips. Cut strips into
2 (6½" x 54½") side borders and
2 (6½" x 34½") top and bottom
borders.

• From remainder, cut 4 (2¼"-wide)
strips lengthwise for binding.

• From remainder, cut 20 (4½")
squares (C).

BLOCK ASSEMBLY

**1. Traditional piecing for half-
square triangles:** Join 1 tan triangle
and 1 black triangle to form half-
square triangle unit A *(A Unit
Assembly Diagrams)*. Make 8 A units.

**Quick piecing for half-square trian-
gles:** On wrong side of 1 (2⅞"-wide)
tan strip, draw 2⅞" squares. Draw
alternating diagonals in squares.
Match tan strip with 1 black strip,
with right sides facing. Stitch ¼"
away from diagonal drawn lines on
both sides. Cut on all drawn lines.
Open out and press seam allowance
to black side. Make 160 black-and-
tan A half-square triangle units.

2. Referring to *Block Assembly
Diagram*, lay out 8 A units, 2 tan B
squares, 2 black-and-tan B squares,
and 1 floral C square. Join pieces as
shown to complete 1 Old Maid's
Puzzle block *(Block Diagram)*.

3. Make 20 Old Maid's Puzzle
blocks.

*A Unit Assembly
Diagrams*

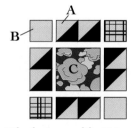

Block Assembly Diagram

Block Diagram

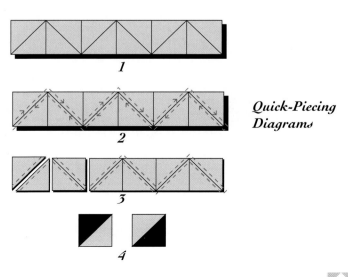

*Quick-Piecing
Diagrams*

QUILT ASSEMBLY

1. Lay out blocks in 5 horizontal rows of 4 blocks each, as shown in *Quilt Top Assembly Diagram.* Join into rows; join rows to complete center.

2. Measure quilt to ensure that borders will fit; trim if necessary. Add 1½" x 32½" tan borders to top and bottom of quilt. Add 1½" x 42½" tan borders to sides of quilt.

3. Add 6½" x 34½" floral borders to top and bottom of quilt. Add 6½" x 54½" floral borders to sides of quilt.

QUILTING AND FINISHING

1. Divide backing fabric into 2 (1½-yard) lengths. Cut 1 piece in half lengthwise. Sew 1 narrow panel to 1 side of wide panel. Press seam allowances toward narrow panel. Seam will run horizontally. Other panel is extra and may be used to make a hanging sleeve.

2. Layer backing, batting, and quilt top; baste. Quilt as desired. Quilt shown was meander-quilted in outer light areas and block dark areas; rose pattern appears in block intersections and outer borders.

3. Join 2¼"-wide black floral print strips into 1 continuous piece for straight-grain French-fold binding. Add binding to quilt.

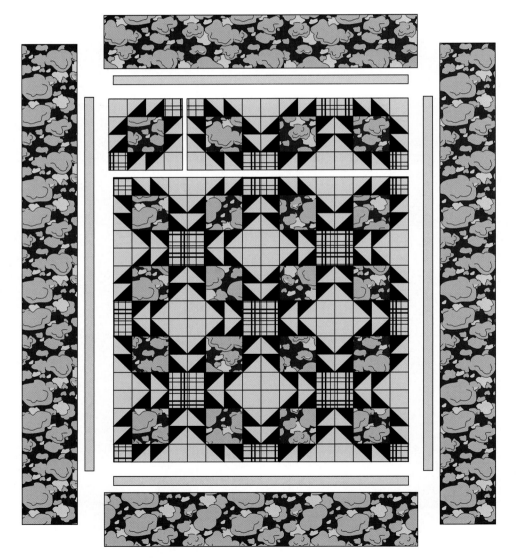

Quilt Top Assembly Diagram

Log Cabin

 othing says cozy quite like a flannel Log Cabin quilt. It works well in plaids, as shown here, or in floral prints for a more feminine look. And here's your opportunity to use up any leftover strips from other projects.

Finished Size: 60" x 60"
Blocks: 36 (10") Log Cabin Blocks

MATERIALS

¼ yard solid red for block centers

2 yards (or 16 fat eighths* or 8 fat quarters**) assorted light prints and plaids

2¼ yards (or 18 fat eighths* or 9 fat quarters**) assorted dark prints and plaids

½ yard solid navy for binding

4 yards fabric for backing (See sidebar on page 34 for optional pieced back.)

Twin-size batting

*Fat eighth = 9" x 22"

**Fat quarter = 18" x 22"

CUTTING

Measurements include ¼ " seam allowances. Cut selvage to selvage, unless otherwise noted.

From solid red, cut:

• 3 (2½"-wide) strips. Cut strips into 36 (2½") squares for block centers.

From light prints and plaids, cut:

• 85 (1½" x 22") strips.

From dark prints and plaids, cut:

• 100 (1½" x 22") strips.

From solid navy, cut:

• 7 (2¼ "-wide) strips for binding.

BLOCK ASSEMBLY

1. Choose 1 light strip for first log (2). With right sides facing, lay strip atop 1 side of 1 red square (1) and stitch. Trim log even with bottom of red square. Press seam allowance to new log *(Diagram 1)*.

2. Rotate unit so that new log is at bottom. With right sides facing, match same light strip to right edge of red square for log 3. Stitch, trim, and press as before *(Diagram 2)*.

3. Rotate new log to bottom. Match 1 dark strip to the right edge of red square. Stitch, trim, and press *(Diagram 3)*.

4. Rotate new log to bottom. With right sides facing, match same dark strip to right edge of red square. Stitch, trim, and press.

5. Continue in this manner until you have 4 logs on each side of red square. Press to newest log and rotate to bottom to add next strip.

6. Make 36 Log Cabin blocks *(Block Diagram)*.

Diagram 1   *Diagram 2*   *Diagram 3*

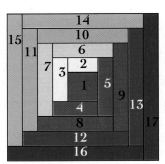

Block Diagram

QUILT ASSEMBLY

Lay out blocks in 6 horizontal rows of 6 blocks each, as shown in *Quilt Top Assembly Diagram*. Join into rows; join rows to complete center.

QUILTING AND FINISHING

1. Divide backing fabric into 2 (2-yard) lengths. Cut 1 piece in half lengthwise. Sew 1 narrow panel to each side of wide panel. Press seam allowances toward narrow panels.
2. Layer backing, batting, and quilt top; baste. Quilt as desired. Quilt shown was outline-quilted in concentric squares.
3. Join 2¼ "-wide navy strips into 1 continuous piece for straight-grain French-fold binding. Add binding to quilt.

Quilt Top Assembly Diagram

Decorative Pieced Back

Kris Bishop found a creative way to piece the back of her quilt. She made a giant Log Cabin block! This worked for Kris because her quilt top is square. Follow the instructions below for a decorative pieced back.

MATERIALS

½ yard solid red for center
8 assorted light and dark prints (See table for yardage.)

CUTTING

From solid red, cut:
• 1 (15½") square for center.

From light and dark prints, cut:
• as shown in table.

Fabric	Log Number	Yardage	Cut
Light 1	2, 3	¼ yard	1 (6½"-wide) strip.
Light 2	6, 7	½ yard	2 (6½"-wide) strips.
Light 3	10, 11	½ yard	2 (6½"-wide) strips; piece as needed.
Light 4	14, 15	¾ yard	3 (6½"-wide) strips; piece as needed.
Dark 1	4, 5	½ yard	2 (6½"-wide) strips.
Dark 2	8, 9	½ yard	2 (6½"-wide) strips.
Dark 3	12, 13	¾ yard	3 (6½"-wide) strips; piece as needed.
Dark 4	16, 17	¾ yard	3 (6½"-wide) strips; piece as needed.

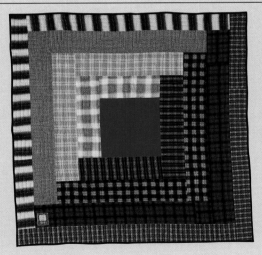

ASSEMBLY

1. Assemble as shown above and, referring to *Block Diagram*, page 32, using (15½") square for center and 6½" strips for logs.
2. Backing should measure 63½". Substitute for 4 yards of backing.

Homespun Pleasures

ary Gray Hart made this cozy nap-size quilt for her brother, John Gray. "The best bonus of quilting," says Mary, "is all the women I have met and gotten to know. We seem to share more than just a hobby; we share basic values of family and friends—the homespun pleasures of life!"

MATERIALS

1¾ yards total (12 to 20 fat
  eighths* or fat quarters**)
  assorted light plaids and prints
  for blocks

2¼ yards total (12 to 20 fat
  eighths* or fat quarters**)
  assorted dark plaids and prints
  for blocks and inner border

1½ yards total 4 to 6 assorted
  dark red prints for border and
  binding

1½ yards total 4 to 6 assorted
  dark plaids for borders

3½ yards fabric for backing

Twin-size batting

Template plastic

Pearl cotton for utility quilting
  (optional)

*Fat eighth = 9" x 22"

**Fat quarter = 18" x 22"

CUTTING

Most blocks have matched fabrics in
them. Some are mixed for a scrappier
look. Make templates, using patterns
A and B at right. Cutting instructions
are for matched blocks, but you may
substitute as desired. Measurements
include ¼" seam allowances. Cut
selvege to selvage, unless otherwise
noted.

**From assorted light plaids and
prints, cut:**

- 11 (1½" x 22") assorted strips for
  Courthouse Steps. From these,
  cut:
  - 17 sets of 2 matching 1½" x 2"
    rectangles.
  - 17 sets of 2 matching 1½" x 4"
    rectangles.
  - 17 sets of 2 matching 1½" x 6"
    rectangles.
- 12 sets of 4 matching As for dark
  star blocks.
- 12 sets of 4 matching 3" squares
  (C) for dark star blocks.
- 6 sets of 4 matching Bs and B rev.
  to make 8 matching points for
  light star blocks.
- 6 (3") squares (C) to match B
  point sets for light star centers.
- 4 different 3" squares for inner
  border corners.

**From assorted dark plaids and
prints, cut:**

- 16 (1½" x 22") assorted strips for
  Courthouse Steps. From these,
  cut:
  - 17 sets of 2 matching 1½" x 4"
    rectangles.
  - 17 sets of 2 matching 1½" x 6"
    rectangles.
  - 17 sets of 2 matching 1½" x 8"
    rectangles.
- 5 (3"-wide) assorted strips. Cut
  strips into random lengths from
  10" to 22". Piece to make 2
  (3" x 53") inner side borders and
  2 (3" x 38") inner top and bottom
  borders.
- 6 sets of 4 matching As for light
  star blocks.
- 6 sets of 4 matching 3" squares for
  light star blocks.
- 12 sets of 4 matching Bs and 4 B
  rev. to make 8 matching points for
  dark star blocks.
- 12 (3") squares to match B point
  sets for dark star centers.

From assorted dark red prints, cut:

- 17 assorted 2" squares for
  Courthouse Steps centers.
- 6 (1½"-wide) assorted strips. Cut
  strips into random lengths from
  12" to 30". Piece to make 2 (1½" x
  58") middle side borders and
  2 (1½" x 45") middle top and
  bottom borders.
- 7 (2¼"-wide) assorted strips for
  straight-grain binding.

From assorted dark plaids, cut:

- 7 (8"-wide) assorted strips. Piece
  to make 2 (8" x 75") outer side
  borders and 2 (8" x 45") outer top
  and bottom borders.

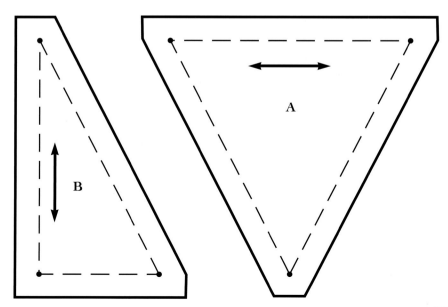

54-40 or Fight Block Assembly

1. Join 1 dark B and 1 matching dark B rev. to each side of 1 light A. Make 4 matching units.

2. Lay out 4 matching A/B units, 1 matching dark C, and 4 matching light Cs as shown in *54–40 or Fight Block Assembly Diagram.* Press seam allowances toward C squares. Join into rows; join rows to complete dark star with light background.

3. Referring to *Block Diagrams,* make 12 dark stars with light backgrounds and 6 light stars with dark backgrounds.

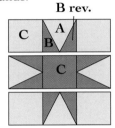

54-40 or Fight Block Assembly Diagram

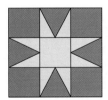 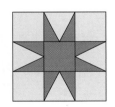

Light Star Block Diagram   *Dark Star Block Diagram*

Courthouse Steps Block Assembly

1. Join 1 set of light 1½" x 2" rectangles to opposite sides of 1 (2") red print square. Press seam allowances away from center square. Join 1 set of dark 1½" x 4" rectangles to opposite side of this unit. Referring to *Courthouse Steps Block Assembly Diagram,* continue with increasing set lengths, alternating light and dark sets and stopping with third set of

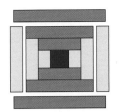

Courthouse Steps Block Assembly Diagram

Courthouse Steps Block Diagram

dark rectangles. Press seam allowances away from center.

2. Make 17 Courthouse Steps blocks as shown in *Courthouse Steps Block Diagram.*

Quilt Top Assembly

1. Join 3 dark star blocks with 2 Courthouse Steps blocks as shown in *Row A Assembly Diagram.* Make 4 of Row A. Press seam allowances toward star blocks.

2. Join 3 Courthouse Steps blocks and 2 light star blocks as shown in *Row B Assembly Diagram.* Press seam allowances toward star blocks. Make 3 of Row B.

3. Referring to photo, join rows to complete quilt center.

4. Join 3" x 53" dark inner borders to each side of quilt. Press seam allowances toward borders. Join 1 (3") light square to each end of 3" x 38" dark top and bottom borders. Add borders to quilt, matching seams. Press as before.

5. Add 1 (1½" x 58") red print border to each side of quilt. Add 1 (1½" x 45") red print border to quilt top and bottom.

6. Add 8" x 45" dark plaid borders to top and bottom of quilt. Add 8" x 75" dark plaid border to each side of quilt.

Quilting and Finishing

1. Divide backing fabric into 2 (1¾-yard) lengths. Cut 1 piece in half lengthwise. Sew 1 narrow panel to each side of wide panel. Press seam allowances toward narrow panels. Seams on backing will run parallel to top and bottom of quilt top.

2. Layer backing, batting, and quilt top; baste. Quilt as desired. Quilt shown is utility-quilted with pearl cotton in overall clamshell design.

3. Join 2¼"-wide assorted red print strips into 1 continuous piece to make approximately 8 yards of French-fold straight-grain binding. Add binding to quilt.

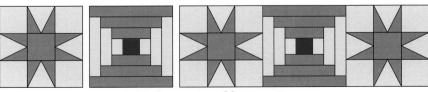

Row A Assembly Diagram

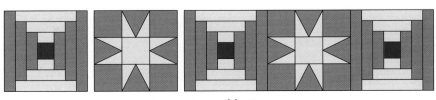

Row B Assembly Diagram

Patriotic Flags

dd folk charm to your home with this handsome wall quilt. Display it as a seasonal accent piece or as the focal point of a room with an Americana decor. Assembly is fast—and fun.

QUILT BY PAT SLOAN

Finished Size: 43" x 34"
Blocks: 4 (9" x 13½") Flag Blocks

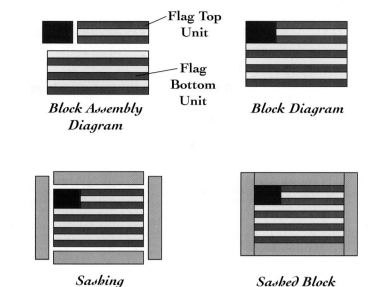

Block Assembly Diagram

Flag Top Unit

Flag Bottom Unit

Block Diagram

Sashing Assembly Diagram

Sashed Block Diagram

MATERIALS

¾ yard red check for flags, border, and binding

¼ yard cream plaid for flags

⅛ yard (or 1 fat eighth*) dark blue stripe for star fields

½ yard blue stripe for border

½ yard light blue plaid for border

1½ yards dark blue-and-red plaid for backing

Crib-size batting

*Fat eighth = 9" x 22"

CUTTING

Measurements include ¼" seam allowances. Cut selvage to selvage, unless otherwise noted.

From red check, cut:
- 6 (1½"-wide) strips for flag stripes.
- 4 (1½"-wide) strips. Cut strips into 2 (1½" x 35½") top and bottom borders and 2 (1½" x 28½") side borders.
- 4 (2¼"-wide) strips for binding.

From cream plaid, cut:
- 5 (1½"-wide) strips for flag stripes.

From dark blue stripe, cut:
- 1 (3½"-wide) strip. Cut strip into 4 (3½" x 4½") rectangles for star field.

From blue stripe, cut:
- 3 (2½"-wide) strips. Cut strips into 4 (2½" x 14") top and bottom sashing strips and 4 (2½" x 13½")

side sashing strips.
- 2 (3½"-wide) strips. Cut strips into 2 (3½" x 14½") side border strips and 2 (3½" x 22") top and bottom border strips.

From light blue plaid, cut:
- 3 (2½"-wide) strips. Cut strips into 4 (2½" x 14") top and bottom sashing strips and 4 (2½" x 13½") side sashing strips.
- 2 (3½"-wide) strips. Cut strips into 2 (3½" x 14½") side border strips and 2 (3½" x 22") top and bottom border strips.

BLOCK ASSEMBLY

Refer to *Block Assembly Diagram* throughout.

1. Join 2 (1½"-wide) red check strips to each side of 1 (1½"-wide) cream plaid strip. Cut strip set into 4 (10"-long) rectangles. Join 1 (3½" x 4½") dark blue rectangle to 1 end of 1 set to make flag top unit. Repeat

to make 4 flag top units.

2. Join 1 (1½"-wide) red check strip to 1 (1½"-wide) cream plaid strip. Repeat to make 4 strip sets.

3. Cut strip sets into 12 (14"-long) rectangles. Join in 4 sets of 3, as shown, to make flag bottom unit.

4. Join top unit to bottom unit (*Block Diagram*). Repeat to make 4 flag blocks.

5. Join 1 blue stripe (2½" x 14") sashing strip to top and bottom of 1 flag block. Join 1 (2½" x 13½") blue stripe sashing strip to sides (*Sashing Assembly Diagram*). Repeat to make 2 blue stripe flag blocks and 2 light blue check flag blocks (*Sashed Block Diagram*).

QUILT ASSEMBLY

1. Lay out sashed flag blocks as shown in *Quilt Top Assembly Diagram* on page 42. Join into rows; join rows.

2. Add 1½" x 35½" red check border strips to top and bottom of quilt. Add red check borders to sides of quilt.

3. Join 1 blue stripe and 1 light blue plaid 3½" x 14½" border strips as shown. Repeat to make 2 borders. Add to sides of quilt. Repeat to add 3½" x 22" top and bottom borders.

QUILTING AND FINISHING

1. Layer backing, batting, and quilt top; baste. Quilt as desired. Quilt shown was machine-quilted with stars in flag, waves in stripes, and looping meander stitching in sashing and borders.

2. Join 2¼"-wide red check strips into 1 continuous piece for straight-grain French-fold binding. Add binding to quilt.

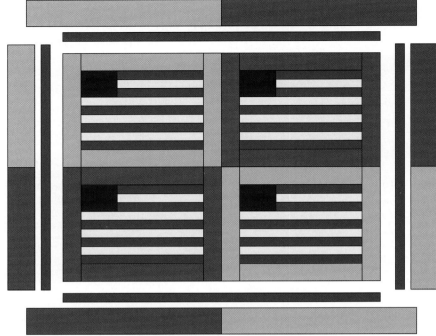

Quilt Top Assembly Diagram

More Ideas

- Give this project to a July baby. Stitch the baby's name and birthdate in a white stripe.
- To make the quilt fit a child's bed, set 3 flags across by 6 flags down.
- Present the quilt to someone in the military. In the white stripes, stitch all the bases where he or she has been stationed.

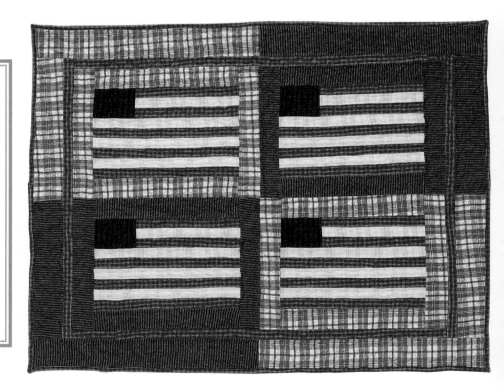

One-Hour Quilt Top

Remember, there are no quilt police. You *can* add a border or two to a novelty print and—voilà—you have a cozy quilt top! This quilt works as a quick gift or as a utility quilt to carry to sporting events or on picnics.

MATERIALS

Use the following yardage requirements as a general guideline to make a lap-size quilt top that requires little or no block piecing.

1½ yards print for quilt center
2 yards coordinating solid for borders and binding

CUTTING

From print:
• Trim selvages. Center area should be about 42"-wide by 54"-long.

From coordinating solid, cut:
• 4 (5½"-wide) lengthwise strips for borders (See text at right for double-border options.)
• 4 (2½"-wide) lengthwise strips for binding.

QUILTS BY RHONDA RICHARDS; QUILTED BY NEW TRADITIONS

PIECED CORNERS

To add interest to your design, make a suitable quilt block for the corners. This dairy-oriented print seemed to call for a Churn Dash block in each corner.

FABRIC (BELOW): NICK AND NORA FLANNEL, "BLUE DAIRY FARM"; PATTERN 3557 "DAIRYLAND" BY SHADY CHARACTER FOR SHADOWBOXER

SINGLE BORDER

When a print has only a few colors, a single border in the darkest color works best. Simple allover quilting is appropriate, because fancy designs are lost on a busy print.

FABRIC (RIGHT): NICK AND NORA FLANNEL, "PINK DREAM DATE" BY SHADY CHARACTER FOR SHADOWBOXER

DOUBLE BORDER

If the print has many colors or a busy look, you may need to frame it with 2 borders. As a general rule, use the darker border on the outside. To get a 5"-wide finished border, use a 2"-wide inner border and a 3"-wide outer border. Use leftovers to piece the backing.

FABRIC (RIGHT): NICK AND NORA FLANNEL, "WHITE BEDTIME STORY"; PATTERN 3503 "BEDTIME STORY" BY SHADY CHARACTER FOR SHADOWBOXER

Sweethearts

Since flannel stretches a little more than other woven cottons, many quilters find foundation piecing an ideal option. Lauren Caswell Brooks used a collection of pastel fat quarters to make this sweet quilt. The size and the colors make it an ideal baby gift.

Finished Size: 30½" x 40½"
Blocks: 18 (5") Heart Blocks,
17 Setting Squares

MATERIALS

10 fat quarters* (or 1½ yards total) assorted yellow, blue, and green pastel plaids and stripes for blocks

2 fat quarters* [use more for variety] (or ½ yard total) assorted cream stripes and plaids for block background

½ yard blue floral for border

1¾ yards cream stripe for binding and backing

Crib-size batting

*Fat quarter = 18" x 22"

CUTTING

Measurements include ¼" seam allowances. Cut selvage to selvage, unless otherwise noted.

From assorted yellow, blue, and green pastel plaids and stripes, cut:

• 12 (1½"-wide) strips for blocks.
• 17 (5½") squares for setting squares.

From assorted cream stripes and plaids, cut:

• 18 (4") squares. Cut squares in half diagonally to make 36 half-square triangles (#8 and #9 on pattern).
• 5 (4") squares. Cut squares in quarters diagonally to make 20 quarter-square triangles (#1 on pattern). You will have 2 extra.
• 18 (2½") squares. Cut squares in half diagonally to make 36 half-square triangles (#10 and #11 on pattern).

From blue floral, cut:

• 4 (3¼"-wide) strips. Cut strips into 2 (3¼" x 35½") strips for side borders and 2 (3½" x 31") strips for top and bottom borders.

From cream stripe, cut:

• 1¼ yard for backing.
• 4 (2¼"-wide) strips for binding.

BLOCK ASSEMBLY

1. Trace or photocopy foundation-piecing pattern. You will need one for each block, for total of 18.

2. Place wrong side of cream fabric for #1 against underneath side of #1 on foundation. Place colored fabric for area #2, with right sides facing, on first fabric piece. Align raw edges of fabric pieces so that they extend ¼" beyond stitching line that joins #1 and #2. Working from right side of paper, use short machine stitch and sew along line between #1 and #2. Trim seam allowances as needed. Open out fabric #2 so that it covers area #2, trim excess from strip, and finger-press seam.

3. Place next fabric for area #3 with right sides facing atop first and

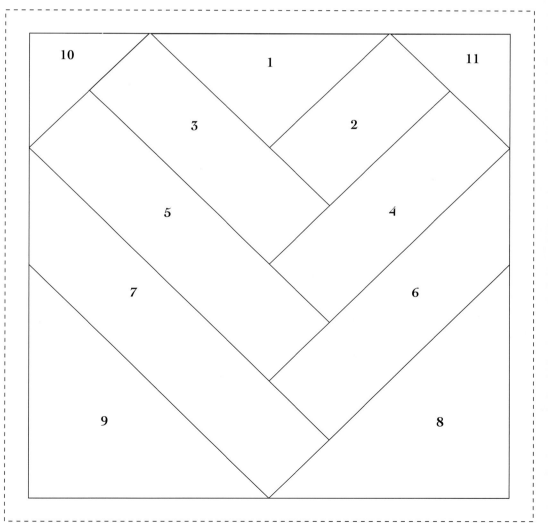

Sweethearts Foundation-Piecing Pattern
Note: Pattern is already reversed, since you will be working from the wrong side.
Leisure Arts grants permission to photocopy this page for personal use only.

second pieces so that seam allowances extend ¼" beyond next stitching line. Stitch along line and trim seam allowance. Open out piece, trim excess from strip, and finger-press.

4. Continue in this manner, adding pieces in numerical order, until all areas on foundation are covered. Right side of fabric design will be formed on wrong side of paper foundation. Trim excess fabric and paper along outer dashed line of paper foundation *(Block Diagram)*.

5. Make 18 Heart blocks. Remove paper from wrong side of block.

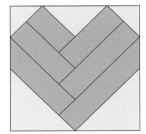

Block Diagram

QUILT ASSEMBLY

1. Lay out heart blocks and setting squares as shown in *Row Assembly Diagrams*. Join into rows as shown in photo; join rows to complete center.

2. Join 1 (3¼" x 35½") blue floral strip to each side of quilt. Add top and bottom borders.

QUILTING AND FINISHING

1. Layer backing, batting, and quilt top; baste. Quilt as desired. Quilt shown was wave-quilted in-the-ditch in heart blocks with meander quilting in block background. Setting blocks feature single looped hearts, with continuous looped hearts in border.

2. Join 2¼"-wide cream stripe strips into 1 continuous piece for straight-grain French-fold binding. Add binding to quilt.

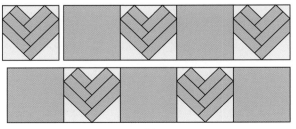

Row Assembly Diagrams

Make Your Cat a Quilt

It's no secret that cats (or dogs, for that matter) love quilts. If you have a problem with your pet shedding on your "good" quilts, consider making him one of his own.

Chances are, your pet has a favorite place to nap—on the couch, in a recliner, or at the foot of your bed. The left-behind fur can seem impossible to remove, even with the help of masking tape or a minivacuum.

I found that the easiest solution to this problem was to make my cats their own quilts. People laugh when I tell them this, but I've saved my sofas and spared myself many headaches when cleaning.

Keep in mind that your pet won't care if your seams don't match perfectly or if your quilting lines aren't even. In fact, you don't even have to make quilt blocks at all! Here are some ideas I've used:

• Check out the remnant bin at your favorite fabric store. That's where I found the flannel remnant shown on this page. Simply machine-quilt the piece in straight lines and bind it. I call this a Kitty Utility Quilt.

• Protect your den sofa with a decorative piece, since this room is a popular family gathering place. Choose a simple pattern, such as *Roman Stripe* on page 56. You can use the 30 extra units left over from that quilt to make a simple 5 x 6 block setting.

• Join a collection of blocks that didn't make it into a project to make your pet a quilt.

• Remember that care is easy for a pet quilt. I simply machine-wash my cats' quilts with regular detergent and then dry them. By washing them at least once a month, I eliminate smells and lower the chance of my pets getting hair balls.

Checkerboard Stars

Whether you are sleeping under the open night sky or only dreaming of the great outdoors from your warm bed, this star quilt will keep you snug. A solid background sets off the scrappy blocks.

Finished Size: 54" x 66"
Blocks: 20 (9") Checkerboard Star Blocks

MATERIALS

3 yards winter white for background and border (3¼ yards for unpieced borders)
20 fat eighths* (or 2 yards total) assorted medium and dark prints and plaids for blocks
4¾ yards red check for backing and binding
Twin-size batting
*Fat eighth = 9" x 22"

CUTTING

Measurements include ¼" seam allowances. Cut selvage to selvage, unless otherwise noted.

From winter white, cut:
- 6 (2"-wide) strips. Piece to make 2 (2" x 65") side borders and 2 (2" x 53") top and bottom borders. If you prefer unpieced borders, cut 4 (2"-wide) strips from 2 yards of alternate yardage and trim to above lengths. Use remainder for pieces below.
- 16 (2¾"-wide) strips. Cut strips into 80 (2¾") squares (A) and 80 (2¾" x 5") rectangles (B).
- 13 (3½"-wide) strips. Cut strips into 49 (3½" x 9½") sashing strips.

From assorted medium and dark prints and plaids:
- **Choose 2 contrasting fabrics for star blocks.**
  - **From Fabric 1**, cut 4 (2") squares (C) for checkerboard and 8 (2¾") squares (A) for star points.
  - **From Fabric 2**, cut 5 (2") squares (C) for checkerboard.
  - Repeat to cut 20 sets.
- **Cut:**
  - 40 (2") squares in sets of 2 for Four-Patch sashing squares.
  - 80 (2⅜") squares in sets of 2. Cut each square in half diagonally to make 160 half-square triangles in sets of 4 for Pinwheel sashing squares.
  - 4 (2") squares for corner squares.

From red check, cut:
- 1 (26") square for bias binding.

NINE-PATCH BLOCK ASSEMBLY

1. Lay out 5 Fabric 2 (2") squares (C) and 4 Fabric 1 (2") squares (C) as shown in *Nine-Patch Block Assembly Diagram*.
2. Join into rows; join rows to complete 1 Nine-Patch block *(Nine-Patch Block Diagram)*.

STAR BLOCK ASSEMBLY

1. Referring to *Diagonal Seams Diagrams*, position 1 A square atop 1 B rectangle. Stitch diagonally, trim, and press open. Repeat on opposite end with matching A to make 1 Goose Chase unit. Make 4 matching Goose Chase units.
2. Referring to *Star Block Assembly Diagram*, join 1 Goose Chase unit to each side of 1 Nine-Patch block. Join 1 winter white A square to each end of remaining Goose Chase units. Join to top and bottom of block.

Nine-Patch Block Assembly Diagram

Diagonal Seams Diagrams

Nine-Patch Block Diagram

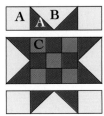

Star Block Assembly Diagram

Star Block Diagram

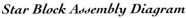

3. Make 20 Checkerboard Star blocks (*Star Block Diagram*, page 48).

FOUR-PATCH BLOCK ASSEMBLY

1. Choose 2 sets of 2 (2") squares. Join as shown in *Four-Patch Block Assembly Diagram* to make 1 Four-Patch sashing square.

2. Make 10 Four-Patch sashing squares (*Four-Patch Block Diagram*).

PINWHEEL BLOCK ASSEMBLY

1. Choose 2 sets of 4 half-square triangles. Referring to *Pinwheel Block Assembly Diagrams*, join 1 triangle from each set together to make 1 square. Make 4 squares. Join as shown to make 1 Pinwheel sashing square.

2. Make 20 Pinwheel sashing squares (*Pinwheel Block Diagram*).

QUILT ASSEMBLY

1. Alternate 5 sashing squares and 4 sashing strips, placing sashing squares as shown in Sashing Row of *Quilt Top Assembly Diagram*. Join to make 1 row. Make 6 Sashing Rows.

2. Alternate 5 sashing strips and 4 blocks. Join to make 1 Block Row. Make 5 Block Rows.

3. Alternate sashing rows and block rows, placing sashing squares in their proper positions. Join rows to complete center.

4. Add winter white 2" x 65" border strips to sides of quilt. Add 1 (2") corner square to ends of remaining border strips. Add to top and bottom of quilt.

QUILTING AND FINISHING

1. Divide backing fabric into 2 (2-yard) lengths. Cut 1 piece in half lengthwise. Sew 1 narrow panel to 1 side of wide panel. Press seam allowances toward narrow panel. Remaining panel is extra and may be used to make hanging sleeve.

2. Layer backing, batting, and quilt top; baste. Quilt as desired. Quilt shown was grid-quilted.

3. Make 7 yards of 2¼"-wide French-fold bias binding from 26" red check square. Add binding to quilt.

Four-Patch Block Assembly Diagram

Four-Patch Block Diagram

Pinwheel Block Assembly Diagram 1

Pinwheel Block Assembly Diagram 2

Pinwheel Block Diagram

Quilt Top Assembly Diagram

Grandmother's Flower Garden

*F*or a portable project, start a *Grandmother's Flower Garden* quilt, using the English paper-piecing method. This pattern dates back at least two centuries. Other names include *Honeycomb, Country Tile,* and *Martha Washington's Garden.*

Finished Size: 33" x 35"
Blocks: 23 (1½"-diameter)
Grandmother's Flower Garden Blocks

MATERIALS

⅛ yard (or fat eighth*) light print for flower centers
½ yard total or 23 (5" x 7") pieces assorted prints for flowers
½ yard green for path
1 yard green-and-tan stripe for background
¾ yard green floral for border
⅝ yard different green floral for binding
1 yard fabric for backing
Crib-size batting
* Fat eighth = 9" x 22"

CUTTING

Measurements include ¼" seam allowances. Cut selvage to selvage, unless otherwise noted.

From light print, cut:
• 23 As for flower centers.

From assorted prints, cut:
• 23 sets of 6 As for flowers.

From green, cut:
• 162 As for path.

From green-and-tan stripe, cut:
• 1 (25½" x 27½") rectangle for background.

From green floral, cut:
• 4 (4½"-wide) border strips.

From second green floral, cut:
• 4 (2¼"-wide) strips for binding.

BLOCK ASSEMBLY

1. Join 6 print As to 1 light A as shown in *Block Assembly Diagram* to form flower. See page 55 for English paper-piecing instructions.
2. Make 23 flowers.
3. Arrange flowers as desired. Add green As as shown in photo to form path.

QUILT ASSEMBLY

1. Center flower unit on background rectangle. Appliqué in place.
2. Center 1 border strip on each side of quilt. Join to quilt and miter corners.

QUILTING AND FINISHING

1. Layer backing, batting, and quilt top; baste. Quilt as desired. Quilt shown was utility-quilted around each flower and outside of path; centers are outline-quilted and border has an interlocking heart pattern.
2. Join 2¼"-wide green floral strips into 1 continuous piece for straight-grain French-fold binding. Add binding to quilt.

Block Assembly Diagram

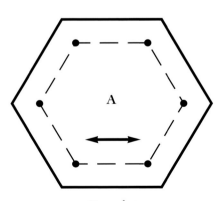

Template

English Paper Piecing

Use this method to make *Grandmother's Flower Garden* blocks.

1. Using pattern A on page 53, trace and cut paper template **without seam allowances** from freezer paper for each hexagon design. (You will need 323 hexagons for quilt shown here.)

To cut several freezer-paper shapes quickly, fanfold the paper to create several layers. Trace the template on the top layer only. Then pin or staple all the layers together to keep them from shifting; or touch the center quickly with the tip of a hot, dry iron. Cut out the templates through all the layers (Photo A).

2. With shiny side of freezer paper against wrong side of fabric, press paper templates to pieces of fabrics, using dry iron and wool setting. Make sure fabric pieces are at least ¼" larger than paper templates.

3. Use rotary cutter and ruler to cut out each shape ¼" beyond paper edge (Photo B).

4. Working with paper side up, fold seam allowance over paper edge. Using running stitch, baste seam allowance to wrong side, stitching through paper (Photo C).

5. With right sides facing and folded edges aligned, whipstitch pieces together. Pull thread through and reinsert needle in folds next to previous stitch, looping thread over folded edges (Photo D). Make tiny stitches, approximately ¹⁄₁₆" to ⅛" apart, and sew from corner to corner. Knot thread or make backstitches to secure whipstitched seam at beginning and end.

6. Remove basting stitches and freezer paper.

Note: We used contrasting thread in photos so that stitches would be visible, but matching thread is preferable.

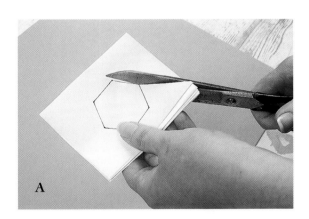

A

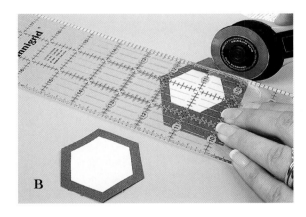

B

C

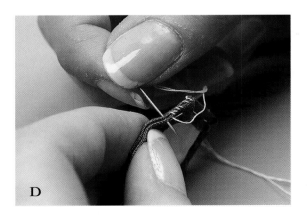

D

Roman Stripe

indy Cooper made this Roman Stripe quilt for her husband, Robert. "He enjoys being cozy while watching television," says Cindy. "I chose these rich tones because they remind me of his flannel shirts."

Finished Size: 56" x 65"
Blocks: 270 (3") Roman Stripe Blocks

MATERIALS

¾ yard medium brown floral for blocks and outer border
⅛ yard each of 12 assorted darks
⅛ yard each of 12 assorted mediums
⅛ yard each of 12 assorted lights
¾ yard dark plaid for inner border
4 yards light brown floral for backing and binding
Twin-size batting

CUTTING

Measurements include ¼" seam allowances. Cut selvage to selvage, unless otherwise noted.

From medium brown floral, cut:
• 5 (4½"-wide) strips. Piece to make 2 (4½" x 57½") side borders and 2 (4½" x 56½") top and bottom borders.

From each ⅛ yard of assorted darks, mediums, and lights, cut:
• 2 (1½"-wide) strips for blocks.

From dark plaid, cut:
• 5 (2"-wide) strips. Piece to make 2 (2" x 54½") side borders and 2 (2" x 48½") top and bottom borders.

BLOCK ASSEMBLY

1. Join 1 dark, 1 medium, and 1 light strip as shown in *Strip Set Diagrams*. Make 23 strip sets.
2. Cut each strip set into 12 (3½") squares *(Block Diagram)*. You will have some extras.

QUILT ASSEMBLY

1. Lay out blocks in 18 horizontal rows of 15 blocks each, as shown in *Quilt Top Assembly Diagram* on page 58 or as desired. Join into rows; join rows to complete center.
2. Join 2" x 54½" dark plaid border strips to each side of quilt. Add top and bottom borders.
3. Join 4½" x 57½" medium brown border strips to sides of quilt. Add top and bottom borders.

QUILTING AND FINISHING

1. Divide backing fabric into 2 (2-yard) lengths. Cut 1 piece in half lengthwise. Sew 1 narrow panel to 1 side of wide panel. Press seam allowances toward narrow panel. Remaining panel is extra and may be used to make a hanging sleeve.
2. Layer backing, batting, and quilt top; baste. Quilt as desired. Quilt shown was meander-quilted in an allover leaf pattern.
3. Trim backing to 2" on all sides. Fold in to edge of quilt. Fold in again and stitch in place to make binding, mitering corners.

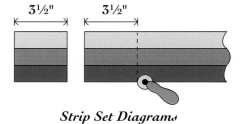

Strip Set Diagrams

Block Diagram

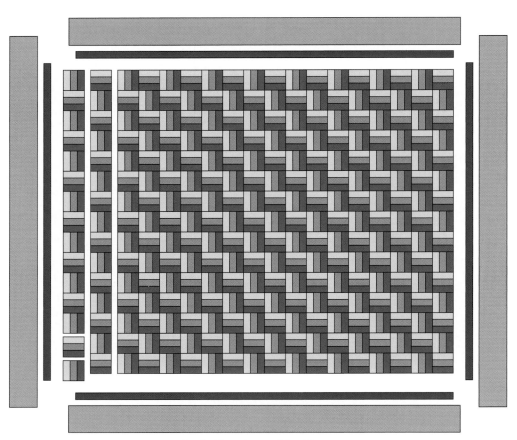

Quilt Top Assembly Diagram

Straight-Grain Binding

Because flannels are so stretchy, you will probably want to use straight-grain French-fold binding for most of your quilts. Not only will it be easier to make and apply than bias binding, but also it can help your quilt hang straighter. (See page 7 for bias binding instructions.)

MAKING BINDING

1. Cut number of strips indicated in instructions.

2. Join strips end to end to make continuous strip. To join 2 strips, layer them perpendicular to each other, with right sides facing. Stitch diagonal seam across strips *(Diagram 1)*. Trim seam allowances to ¼" and press open.

3. Fold binding in half, with wrong sides facing, along top of strip; press.

APPLYING BINDING

Machine-stitch binding to front of quilt first. Begin stitching in middle of any quilt side. Do not trim excess batting and backing until after you stitch binding to quilt.

1. Matching raw edges, lay binding on quilt. Fold down top corner of binding at 45° angle, align raw edges, and pin.

2. Beginning at folded end, stitch binding to quilt, using ¼" seam *(Diagram 2)*. Stop stitching ¼" from corner and backstitch. Remove your quilt from machine.

3. Fold binding strip straight up, away from quilt, to make 45° angle *(Diagram 3)*.

4. Fold binding straight down along next side to be stitched, creating fold that is even with raw edge of previously stitched side.

5. Begin stitching at top edge of new side *(Diagram 4)*. Stitch down this side. Continue until all 4 corners and sides are joined.

FINISHING BINDING

1. Overlap ends of binding over beginning fold and stitch about 2" beyond it. Trim any excess binding.

2. Trim excess batting and backing.

3. Turn binding over raw edge of quilt and slipstitch in place on backing, using thread that matches binding.

4. At each corner, fold binding to form miter *(Diagram 5)*. Stitch miters closed.

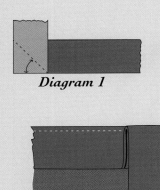

Diagram 1

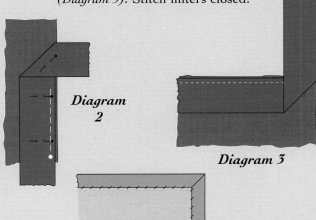

Diagram 2

Diagram 3

Diagram 4

Diagram 5

DESIGNED BY LIZ PORTER; MADE BY RHONDA RICHARDS; QUILTED BY NEW TRADITIONS

Diamond Four-Patch

*I*f you've shied away from diamond shapes because you thought they were difficult, this quilt will change your mind. By using the 60° angle on your rotary-cutting ruler, you'll be whipping out four-patch diamonds one after another!

Finished Size: 63³/₄" x 88"
Blocks: 63 (5¹/₂") Diamond Four-Patch Blocks

MATERIALS

2¹/₄ yards total assorted plaids and stripes or 22 (3¹/₄" x 42") strips
3¹/₂ yards yellow print for blocks and binding
1¹/₄ yards yellow plaid for border
5 yards fabric for backing
Twin-size batting

CUTTING

Measurements include ¹/₄" seam allowances. Cut selvage to selvage, unless otherwise noted.

From assorted plaids and stripes, cut:
• 20 (3¹/₄"-wide) strips.

From yellow print, cut:
• 16 (6"-wide) strips for setting diamonds.
• 7 (2¹/₄"-wide) strips for binding.

From yellow plaid, cut:
• 6 (6"-wide) strips for border.

BLOCK ASSEMBLY

1. Join 1 light and 1 dark 3¹/₄" strip along long sides, offsetting by 1¹/₂". Make 11 strip sets.
2. Using 60° angle on your rotary-cutting ruler, make parallel cuts 3¹/₄" wide as shown in *Diagram 1*. Cut strip sets into 126 Two-Patch Diamond Units.
3. Join 2 Two-Patch Diamond Units into 1 Four-Patch Diamond Block, as shown in *Block Assembly Diagram*. Make 63 Four-Patch Diamond Blocks *(Block Diagram)*.
4. Using 60° angle on your rotary-cutting ruler, cut 80 (6"-wide) diamonds from yellow print as shown in *Diagram 2*.
5. Using 60° angle on your rotary-cutting ruler, cut 36 (6"-wide) diamonds from yellow plaid as shown *Diagram 3* for outer setting diamonds.

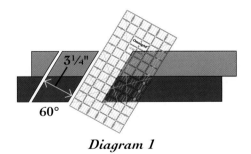

Diagram 1

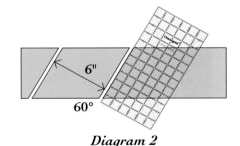

Diagram 2

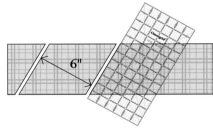

Diagram 3

Block Assembly **Block Diagram**
Diagram

QUILT ASSEMBLY

1. Referring to *Quilt Top Assembly Diagram,* lay out blocks. Join into diagonal rows; join rows.

2. Using long rotary-cutting ruler, trim outer diamonds, leaving ¼" seam allowance. Or you may trim quilt top after quilting is complete.

QUILTING AND FINISHING

1. Divide backing fabric into 2 (2½-yard) lengths. From 1 panel, cut 25"-wide lengthwise piece. Sew 25"-wide panel to 1 side of wide panel. Press seam allowance toward narrow panel. Remaining narrow panel is extra.

2. Layer backing, batting, and quilt top; baste. Quilt as desired. Quilt shown has diamond-shaped stencil over each block.

3. Join 2¼"-wide strips into 1 continuous piece for straight-grain French-fold binding. Add binding to quilt.

Quilt Top Assembly Diagram

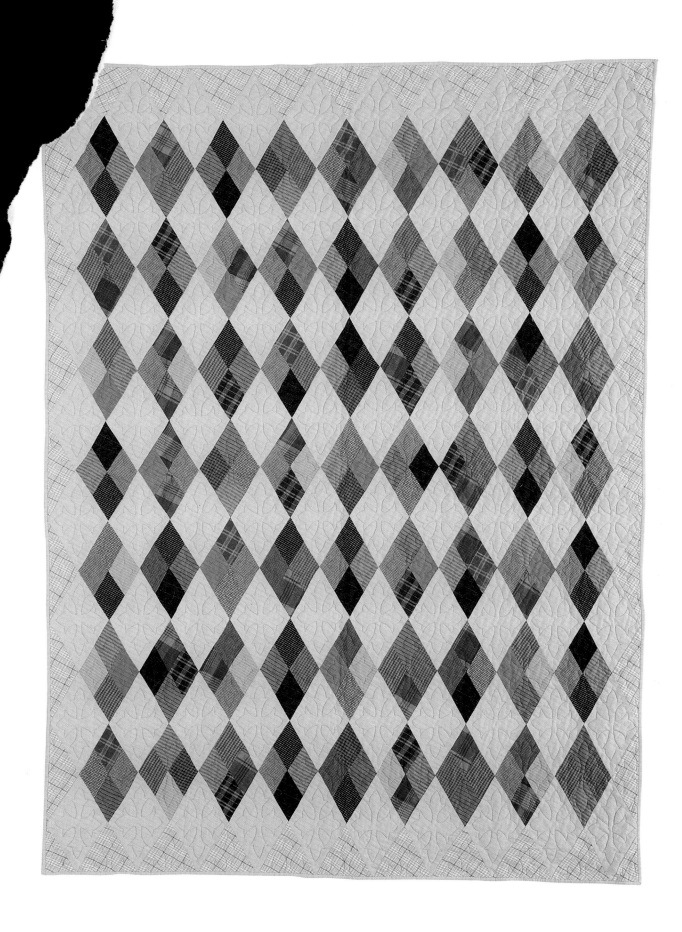

Resources

ontact the following companies for free catalogs or product information.

GENERAL QUILT SUPPLIES AND FABRIC

Benartex
www.benartex.com

Connecting Threads
P.O. Box 8940
Vancouver, WA 98668-8940
1-800-574-6454

Hancock's of Paducah
3841 Hinkleville Road
Paducah, KY 42001
1-800-845-8723
fax: (502) 443-2164
www.Hancocks-Paducah.com

Keepsake Quilting™
P.O. Box 1618
Centre Harbor, NH 03226
1-800-865-9458
www.keepsakequilting.com

Oxmoor House
1-800-633-4910
www.oxmoorhouse.com

The Quilt Farm
P.O. Box 7877
Saint Paul, MN 55107
1-800-435-6201
www.quiltfarm.com

ROTARY-CUTTING MATS AND RULERS

Omnigrid, Inc.
1560 Port Drive
Burlington, WA 98233
1-800-755-3530